"Every good
and perfect gift
is from above."

James 1:17

From: The Greer's
Christmas 2004

Published by Barbour Books, an imprint of Barbour Publishing, Inc., P.O. Box 719, Uhrichsville, Ohio 44683 www.barbourbooks.com

Member of the
Evangelical Christian
Publishers Association

Printed in China.
5 4 3

O Come,
All Ye Faithful

COLLEEN REECE
AND JULIE REECE-DEMARCO

DayMaker
GREETING BOOKS

O COME, ALL YE FAITHFUL

Celebrating the Birth of Christ

CHRISTMAS is a time for the faithful to gather. Millions of us rush home for the holidays. Those who may not usually attend church assemble to worship and celebrate the birth of Christ. We hear songs such as "There's no Place Like Home for the Holidays" and "I'll be Home for Christmas" on radio and TV. We meet for Christmas caroling, parties, and strengthening bonds with family, friends, and God. Our need to gather, especially if we are far away physically, emotionally, or spiritually from those we love—or from God— is often most keenly felt at this time of year.

No one knows when the "coming home" custom began. We do know that on the first Christmas, Joseph and Mary traveled the long, weary miles from Nazareth to Joseph's hometown of Bethlehem, where Jesus was born.

*If you cannot be with those you love this year, may you be blessed with good memories and the Presence of One Who loves you:
our Lord Jesus Christ.*

ADESTE FIDELES
(O Come, All Ye Faithful)

O come, all ye faithful,
Joyful and triumphant,
O come ye, O come ye,
To Bethlehem.
Come and behold Him,
Born the King of Angels
O come, let us adore Him,
O come, let us adore Him,
O come, let us adore Him,
Christ, the Lord!

ORIGIN OF HYMN

O Come, All Ye Faithful" is one of the world's most popular Christmas carols. Legend says it was written long ago by an unknown author, and first sung during the thirteenth century—about the same time churches were beginning to use manger scenes to honor Christmas and the birth of Jesus.

More recent information disagrees with the legend. It indicates *Adeste Fideles* was written about 1742, by an Englishman named John Francis Wade, who was employed at the Roman Catholic Center in Douay, France. In 1841, Frederick Oakeley translated the hymn into English. In 1852, Oakely again translated the carol, this time into the English words we know today, "O Come, All Ye Faithful."

The author had no way of knowing the inspiring words would live on and that we would be singing them in the twenty-first century. Today this beloved carol continues to offer an invitation—in over 120 languages—to come and behold the Son of God.

JOYFUL AND TRIUMPHANT

Silent Night

MEGAN gazed through tear-filled eyes at the blurred colored lights covering the large tree on campus. Christmas had always been her favorite time of year. After she moved out of state to attend college three years ago, the old family traditions took on even more meaning. Each December, she struggled to focus on finals, excited that her six hundred mile trek home was just around the corner.

She would hop in the car, roll the windows partially down (despite the sub-freezing temperatures) and sing her way home to the Christmas songs blaring on the stereo.

It didn't matter what time she finally rolled in to the large family farm, Megan knew her mom would have hot cider on the stove and some mouth-watering Christmas treat ready to pull from the oven. Her siblings would gather from their homes, spouses and children in tow, and the festivities would begin. Amidst the chaotic swirl of colors, noises, smells and songs, Megan especially treasured one tradition.

The youngest of five children, Megan reminisced about the year she turned four. Her siblings loaded the sleds and headed for the big hill up the road. She couldn't wait for her turn to zip down the large slope.

Her hopes were crushed by her mother's words. "I'm sorry, Meg, you're just too little for that big hill. Maybe in a couple of years."

"I never get to do anything," she muttered. "Why couldn't you have had me first?"

That night her father snuck into her room, long after the sun had set. "Put on your warmest clothes and follow me," he whispered.

"But what about the other guys?" she asked, looking around at her sleeping sisters.

"Just you," came her father's quick reply, followed by a wink. Out into the deep snow, Megan followed her father, the full moon illuminating her path. He pulled out a bag, and they set to work making the biggest snowman she had ever seen. Her dad's strong arms lifted her to put on the carrot nose and coal eyes. Putting her down and taking her gloved hand in his, he remarked, "Now don't tell anyone. . . . Won't they be surprised to see who came to visit during the night?" The excitement of her secret sent butterflies through Megan's stomach. Dad placed her on his shoulders and marched to the end of their long driveway. He pointed to the stars in the clear night sky, and as they looked up, began singing "Silent Night" in his deep baritone voice. Singing together, Megan felt encircled by her father's love.

Each year, Dad came to her room on Christmas Eve, and they repeated the ritual. Every year the family wondered about the snowman that magically welcomed Christmas. Reflecting on the memories started Megan's tears anew. It wouldn't happen this year. Dad's sudden heart attack three months ago meant it would never happen again.

I just won't go home this year, Megan told herself. *It would be too painful.* Her explanation to her mom that night, "The drive is too long, and I have a lot of work to do," was met with silence.

The next day, after her last final, she shuffled back to her room. Her thoughts were interrupted by the sound of a horn. Sitting in front of her place was her eldest brother. "You better get a move on if we are going to make it before midnight," he ordered.

"I'm not going," she insisted.

"Now what would all your friends think if I had to pick you up and throw you over my shoulder," he threatened.

Megan wordlessly got her things together. *They don't understand,* she thought. *They don't know about Dad's and my secret.*

· · ·

Megan awoke to the sounds of Christmas and pulled the covers back over her head. *Don't they get that it's Christmas Eve? How can they celebrate without Dad?* she bitterly wondered.

The family went through the daily ritual, including opening one present on Christmas Eve. When it came her turn, Megan's mom pulled out a bag and explained, "Your dad asked that I give this to you on Christmas Eve. You are supposed to open it when you are alone." Megan left the room, amidst the whispers and bewildered glances of her family.

Seated on her bed, she opened the bag and found a wilted carrot, two lumps of coal, a scarf, a tape recorder, and a note: *Meet you in our place. . . . Dad.*

Midnight came. Megan snuck out to the front yard. She looked around, wondering what her dad could have meant. He wasn't coming back. He was dead. In the cold air, she began to make the snowman. As she moved silently around the yard collecting snow, memories of years past flooded her mind. The year the head broke right as they were putting it on top. . .the year of the snowball fight. . .the year she told him she was moving out of state for college. . .the year her long-term boyfriend dumped her. . . . Pictures of the last seventeen years filled her head, frame by frame.

After the snowman was done, she trekked to the end of the driveway. Pursuant to her dad's written note, Megan pushed the play button on the recorder. The night was filled with a deep baritone voice, raised in the strains of "Silent Night."

Megan looked back at the snowman and up into the clear night sky. As on the night when she was four, she felt her dad's love surround her when she lifted her voice to join his, *"Sleep in heavenly peace, Sleep in heavenly peace."*

May this special time of year when hearts and thoughts
turn homeward be filled with blessings and great joy.

CHRISTMAS IN MY HOMETOWN

THE time of year when all things seem to don a friendly glow,
When children's eyes are filled with dreams of stockings in a row.
A time of year for strings of lights and manger scenes nearby,
For candlelight and Christmas trees and songs in rich supply.

The time of year when smiles are bright on each and every face.
Skaters and skiers fill the dark, bringing laughter in its place.
A time of year when loved ones join to hail the Savior's birth
And the world seems a little closer to achieving peace on earth.

When families begin to gather, and carolers make the rounds,
When kitchens are filled with home-baked scents, and heavy snow
    carpets the ground,
When hearts start to open with kindness and no plea for help
    is turned down,
I pause and thank God for my blessings; for it's Christmas in my
    hometown.

COLLEEN L. REECE/JULIE REECE-DEMARCO

LONG WAY FROM
CHRISTMAS

TWENTY-three-year-old Gary lay on his bunk in the middle of a cold early-December New England night. He was about as far from his home in Washington State as he could get and still be in the U.S.A. Never in his life had he felt so low. Christmas loomed ahead, bleak and cheerless. The threat of world tensions hung over the season like a pall. It was the first time Gary had ever been away from his close-knit family during the holiday season. To make matters worse, the wounds inflicted by losing a well-loved president in a recent assassination were fresh.

Ever since he arrived at Officers' Candidate School, Gary had been kept so busy he had little time to do anything except the horrendous tasks his training required. Now he restlessly shifted on his hard bunk, desperately needing sleep but unable to shut down his active brain. He had no hopes of going home, even though his class would be given time off. Both Gary's and his parents' financial resources were drained after his recent college graduation.

He thought of his family and their traditions. It never mattered if snow came early to the small logging town where he and his ancestors had lived for generations. Dad would have already selected the perfect tree to fill one end of the dining room, with its old-fashioned ten-foot ceiling. The large fir, cut on family property behind Gary's home, would be allowed to drip dry on the porch. Carefully packed ornaments would brighten the dark green branches. On Christmas Eve, a kettle of home-made clam chowder and plates of crackers, cheese, and fruitcake would follow the opening of gifts. Not even New England's finest could equal Mom's chowder. Everyone would gather for supper, but this year there would be an empty space at the table. Gary's family would try to pretend all was as usual, but deep in his heart, he knew they would also be hurting.

The lonely officer-in-training sighed. How could he stand to miss the warmth and traditions that surrounded the season celebrating Jesus' birth? The simply, but colorfully decorated homes. The caroling. The bob-sledding, roaring fires, and ice skating. School and church programs. Seeing old friends who returned home from college and out-of-town jobs.

There was much more to miss this year than family and village traditions. The girl he had fallen in love with now wore a carefully-selected diamond on her ring finger. They would be married the following summer.

At last Gary fell into a troubled sleep, interrupted all too soon by the demands of another weary day. He forced himself to concentrate, determined to make his family proud and not be one of the high percentage of classmates who would wash out by the time training ended. Quick prayers helped, but they didn't erase his dread of the empty time between late December and the resumption of classes in January.

Day after endless day, Gary trudged through his routine, trying not to think about the upcoming holidays. Then a message came from his family, short and to the point: *They were sending money for him to fly home for the holidays!*

Not one word hinted of the sacrifice the gift involved. Or how the rest of the family had agreed to keep Christmas presents even more modest than usual in order to afford the most meaningful gift of all, the presence of son and brother.

. . .

Neither Gary nor his family recalls any other gifts given or received that particular year. All remember the special joy that came when a certain plane carrying the happiest young man in the country touched down at Sea-Tac airport bearing precious cargo.

May your greatest gift this Christmas be one from the heart.

COME YE TO BETHLEHEM

DAD, tell us again why we have to walk so far." Five-year-old Joseph's whine reverberated around the hills on the dark night.

"Because, stupid," his eight-year-old sister 'helpfully' told him. "It's a tradition. Besides, you aren't walking; you're shuffling."

Silence resounded once again after the brief interchange. It was pierced by Joseph's next question, "What is a tradition, anyway?"

"Well Son," Joe's father quietly explained, slowing his pace, "When I was a little boy just your age, my father took me to this place on this night every year. We walked the same road we are walking tonight. The same moon and stars shone upon our heads. We visited the same sites and sang the same songs we will this night. Traditions are the way we remember our favorite memories. This tradition helps me remember my father, now that he is gone. It also helps me remember the stories he told about his favorite place."

"Are we going to see Grandpa's favorite place now?" Joseph wanted to know.

"Yes," his sister intervened. "I told you that *last* year. . .and the year before. . .and the year before that."

The stars shone especially brightly on the small hills that marked the small family's way. Upon reaching their destination, a smile brightened the lips of the father. He hastily wiped the tears from his eyes.

"*This* was Grandpa's favorite place?" Joe questioned unbelievingly. "It's not pretty at all, and there is nothing fun to do."

"Oh, but it was the most beautiful place in the world to him, and after you hear his story you may change your mind." Joe's father walked around the small quarters, touching the wood posts and beams. Straw crunched loudly underfoot. He stopped to breathe the air in, closing his eyes, seemingly oblivious to his children chasing each other.

"Joseph, Elisabeth, please join me on this bench." He smiled, motioning for his children to be seated. "I'd like to tell you a story."

"Is it Grandpa's story?" Joe asked with interest.

His father nodded. "On a night like this, but very long ago, my father was hard at work. He had spent many hours in the fields during the day and was herding his sheep with friends when darkness came. As my father and his friends gathered to watch their flocks the story is told that:

LO, *the angel of the Lord came upon them, and the glory of the Lord shone round about them: and they were sore afraid. And the angel said unto them, Fear not: for, behold, I bring you good tidings of great joy, which shall be to all people. For unto you is born this day in the city of David a Saviour, which is Christ the Lord.*

And this shall be a sign unto you; Ye shall find the babe wrapped in swaddling clothes, lying in a manger.

And suddenly there was with the angel a multitude of the heavenly host praising God, and saying, Glory to God in the highest, and on earth peace, good will toward men.

And it came to pass, as the angels were gone away from them into heaven, the shepherds said one to another, Let us now go even unto Bethlehem, and see this thing which is come to pass, which the Lord hath made known unto us.

LUKE 2:9–15

My father and his friends hastily got up and went to see the Saviour, of whom the angels had spoken. He witnessed the Christ child, gathered with his mother, Mary, and father, Joseph. It was the most wonderful night of his life. When he told the story, his face radiated pure joy."

"But Dad, I don't understand," Joseph said, his voice filling with confusion. "I thought *this* was Grandpa's favorite place."

"It is, Joe. This is the place the angels talked about. This is the place where the Christ child lay sleeping. It was here that your grandfather witnessed God's greatest miracle. The Saviour was born in this stable. He was here among the animals. So you see, even though it may not look beautiful to you, it was the place where the most beautiful thing that ever took place occurred."

Silence filled the small area. The father and children sat looking around, recalling the events of the night long ago. When they left, Joseph looked at his father. "Do you think I could bring *my* children here someday?"

May you feel the same awe that the shepherds
experienced that night in the fields.

THE CHRISTMAS SYMBOL

ONLY a manger, cold and bare,
    Only a maiden mild,
Only some shepherds kneeling there,
    Watching a little Child;
And yet that maiden's arms enfold
    The King of heaven above;
And in the Christ Child we behold
    The Lord of life and love.

AUTHOR UNKNOWN

COME AND BEHOLD HIM,
BORN THE KING OF ANGELS

NOW *when Jesus was born in Bethlehem of Judaea in the days of Herod the king, behold, there came wise men from the east to Jerusalem, saying, Where is he that is born King of the Jews? for we have seen his star in the east, and are come to worship him.*

When they had heard the king, they departed; and, lo, the star, which they saw in the east, went before them, till it came and stood over where the young child was. When they saw the star, they rejoiced with exceeding great joy.

And when they were come into the house, they saw the young child with Mary his mother, and fell down, and worshipped him: and when they had opened their treasures, they presented unto him gifts; gold, and frankincense, and myrrh.

MATTHEW 2:1–2, 9–11

over a hay bale a
have moved the

Allison push
way would she le
dim outline of th

"We're stuck,
the door. A faint
What on earth? Th
a cheap glow-in-th
felt her heart warm

"Thanks for re
of the star, she walk
her. *I wonder if Ma
wasn't much older tha
so tired and ready to
Maybe the stable was
that night?* New unc

Allison graduall
welcome straw warr
thought was, *I'm gla
Baby Jesus.*

AS WITH GLADNESS MEN OF OLD

AS with gladness, men of old
Did the guiding star behold,
As with joy they hailed its light
Leading onward, beaming bright,
So, most gracious Lord, may we
Evermore be led to Thee.

As with joyful steps they sped
To that lowly manger bed,
There to bend the knee before
Him Whom heaven and earth adore,
So may we with willing feet
Ever seek Thy mercy seat.

Even with
room to room
plugged in the
the empty room
Mom said.

"Just come
waiting."

Thud. The li
Great. No pho
watching over me.
"Come on, Dog.
still afternoon, it
parka, boots and
leave all the house
from here. People
Allison and M
She finished her ch
the lights flickered
Something furr
realized it was Mac.
a big kerosene lanter

.   .   .

She awakened to a beam of light shining in her face and Dad's anxious voice asking, "Allison, are you all right?"

She sat up. "I'm fine."

Later she would tell Mom and Dad how frightened she'd been and how her fear changed to peace. Most importantly, she would share how God used the star's pale light to echo memories of another Christmas and to remind her of His great gift to the world.

May you receive new understanding
of the Christmas story this holiday season.

A MOUNTAIN BETWEEN

HAVE you ever wanted to go somewhere so badly you'd face any obstacle? If so, you have something in common with a girl who lived in the early 1900s.

Beulah McCullough was in her teens when she got her first teaching job just across a mountain range from her hometown. She quietly accepted her father's edict. There would be no money to bring her home for Christmas vacation.

The school closed for the holidays. Beulah bundled herself into warm clothes and slipped away. No mountain would keep *her* away from home at Christmas—especially the mountain she had hiked and skied for years.

Jesus said, "If you have faith as small as a mustard seed, you can say to this mountain, 'Move from here to there' and it will move. Nothing will be impossible for you" (Matthew 17:20, NIV).

Beulah didn't move a mountain, but she had enough faith in herself and in God to ski across one in winter. People in her hometown still remember the young girl's determination.

May you find courage to conquer the mountains
you face throughout the year.

COMING HOME

MADISON bundled her coat tightly, pulled her hood down over her eyes, and braved the winter wind. Why did she put herself through this senseless Christmas ritual? Every year she vowed: no more presents, no more last-minute shopping, no more late night torture. And every year, she was back downtown, fighting the elements, and wishing she were snug on her couch at home.

This is crazy. I don't even like Christmas. It's not like my nieces and nephews need more stuff, and I certainly don't have any children to buy for.

The damp fog encroached as she made her way from the office to the shopping district. Madison's thoughts matched her gray surroundings. *My vote is to fast-forward from Thanksgiving to New Year's Day.* Her bitterness surprised her. She hadn't always hated Christmas. In the far recesses of her memory, she envisioned a smiling little girl adorned in holiday splendor. *I guess it's just a child's holiday. I must have grown out of it.*

Madison stopped at a corner and pushed the button to cross. Her impatient mutterings for the light to change were interrupted by strains of strangely familiar music. Where was the sound coming from? Her gaze fell on a large, stained-glass window. *A church. Another habit better left to children.*

The light changed, and she hurried toward the shopping mall. Her gift buying progressed as usual, with great speed and little thought but with one difference. She couldn't forget the song. Twice she found herself humming stanzas, and she, Madison Elizabeth Stowe, was *not* a hummer. *I must be spending too many hours in the office. Why can't I get that tune out of my head?* Despite desperate attempts to place the song, she couldn't. It wasn't the radio or television. Not the symphony or a concert. Suddenly she remembered. She must have been about six. It was Christmas Eve, and her parents had taken her to a service. A *church* service.

Delighted with her successful recollection, Madison smiled and continued her shopping. The memories kept coming. In the toy store, she remembered taking some of her many toys to a local hospital one holiday season. In the bookstore, she recounted sitting with her head on her father's lap while he read the Christmas story. The candy shop brought memories of freshly baked treats lovingly handed out by elderly church ladies. Unlike other years, this year's shopping flew by. Madison was almost reluctant to leave when she finished. Her visit to the past had left her warm and happy. *This is what Christmas used to feel like. What changed?*

. . .

When she trekked back toward the office, she passed the church that had started the memories. Familiar songs filled the air. She glanced at her watch and mumbled, "I don't suppose it could hurt to poke my head in." Stepping inside the small stone cathedral, she was amazed at the number of people gathered. The warmth sharply contrasted with the air outside. The group began singing. Madison found herself joining in. Each song brought another memory, and with each memory, Christmas seemed a little more joyful. Somehow in this building she felt as if she were with family.

When the service ended, the pastor approached, extending his hand in greeting. "Welcome home."

Madison glanced at those worshiping around her. She looked up at the picture of Christ in the window. She smiled and responded, "Merry Christmas. It's good to *be* home."

May you be filled with warmth as your heart turns
toward your heavenly home.

SOMETHING FOR YOU

CHRISTMAS wishes to change your
"holly" days to "holy" days.

And now abideth faith, hope, charity, these three;
but the greatest of these is charity.
1 CORINTHIANS 13:13

WISHING YOU
INCREASED FAITH

- a fresh sense of the season's importance
- early morning walks and quiet times so God can speak to
  your heart
- the trust in a child's eyes
- a renewal of spirit
- memories of those who encouraged you to dream

behold

WISHING YOU
ETERNAL HOPE

- rainbows after storms
- winter-dormant roses that contain the promise of new life
- comfort in times of trouble and loss
- promise of a better tomorrow: *Weeping may endure for a night, but joy cometh in the morning (Psalm 30:5).*
- the belief even the smallest prayer will be answered

WISHING YOU
THE SPIRIT OF CHARITY

- warm cookies specially baked for a neighbor or shut-in
- quick prayers for others
- special contributions of time, talent, and treasure
- telephone calls and visits to those who need a listening ear
- taking time to sled or carol despite a full calendar
- anonymous notes and gifts that say, "I love and appreciate you"

*May the blessings of faith, hope, and charity
fill your heart to overflowing.*

CHRIST, THE LORD

A Christmas Blessing

WHETHER it be your childhood home, your current home, or an adopted home, the adage, "There's no place like home for the holidays" holds true. At no time of the year are memories more poignant or treasured.

No matter where you will be spending the holidays, may you be blessed with a season with loved ones around you, warm memories of Christmas past, unexpected carolers bearing treats, an increased awareness of God's faithfulness, and a new appreciation of the season's meaning. Christ's journey to His earthly home is the greatest gift the world has ever known. *For God so loved the world, that he gave his only begotten Son, that whosoever believeth in him should not perish, but have everlasting life (John 3:16).*

May you find true peace and happiness as you respond to God's call to "come, all ye faithful."

CHRIST, THE LORD

The Gift of a Thought

CHRISTMAS is a wonderful time of the year. Yet it cannot:

- heal a broken heart
- reclaim a wayward child
- solve all problems
- ensure everlasting happiness

Jesus can. Without Him, Christmas is just another ordinary day. He is not just the "reason for the season." He is God's Son, the Father's gift of love to the world.

> *This Christmas, may you share your appreciation*
> *and return His love by sharing Jesus with others.*